C Major Scale Book

for cello

Three Octaves

by Cassia Harvey

CHP117
©2012 by C. Harvey Publications All Rights Reserved.
6403 N. 6th Street
Philadelphia, PA 19126
www.charveypublications.com

The C Major Scale Book

1

Cassia Harvey

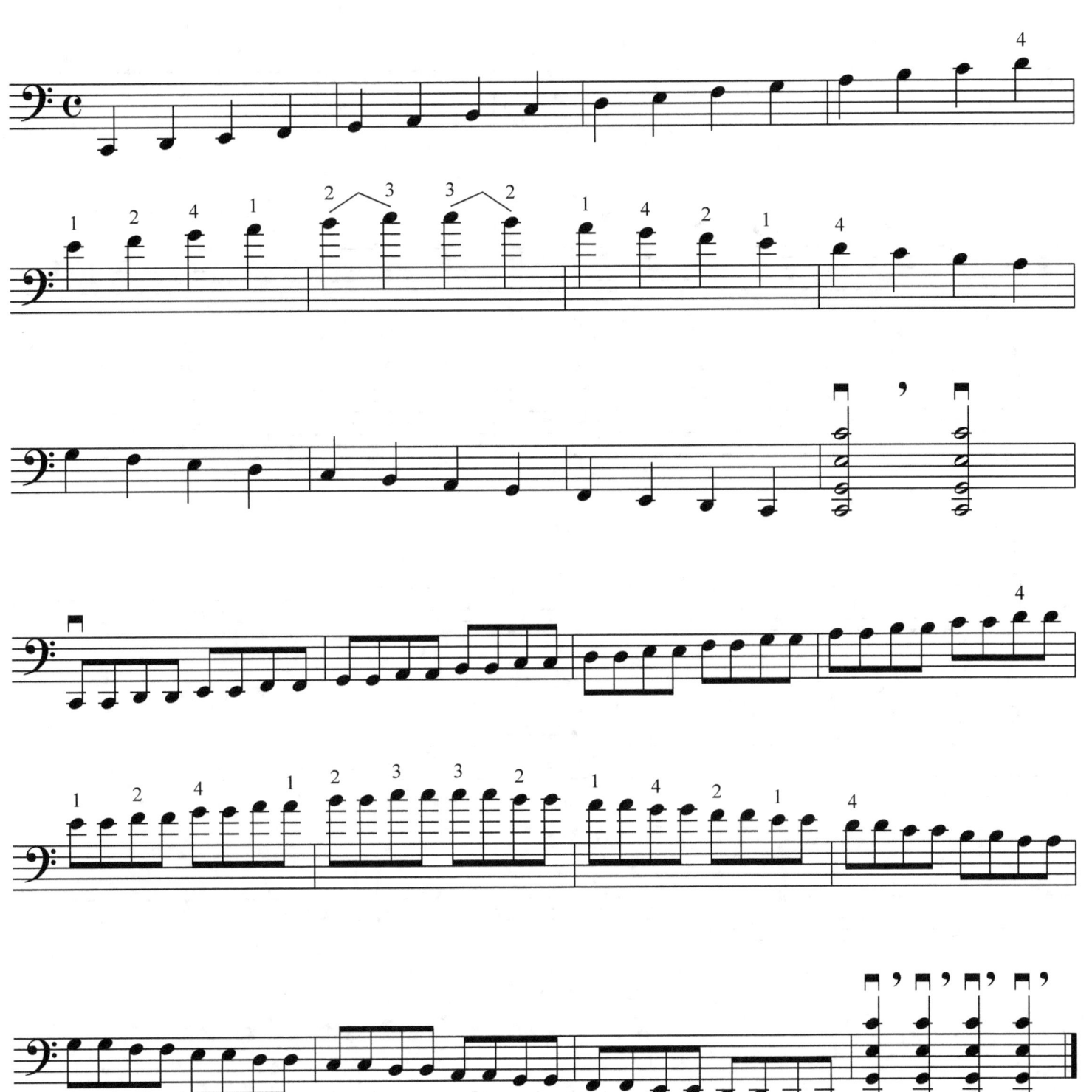

©2012 C. Harvey Publications All Rights Reserved.

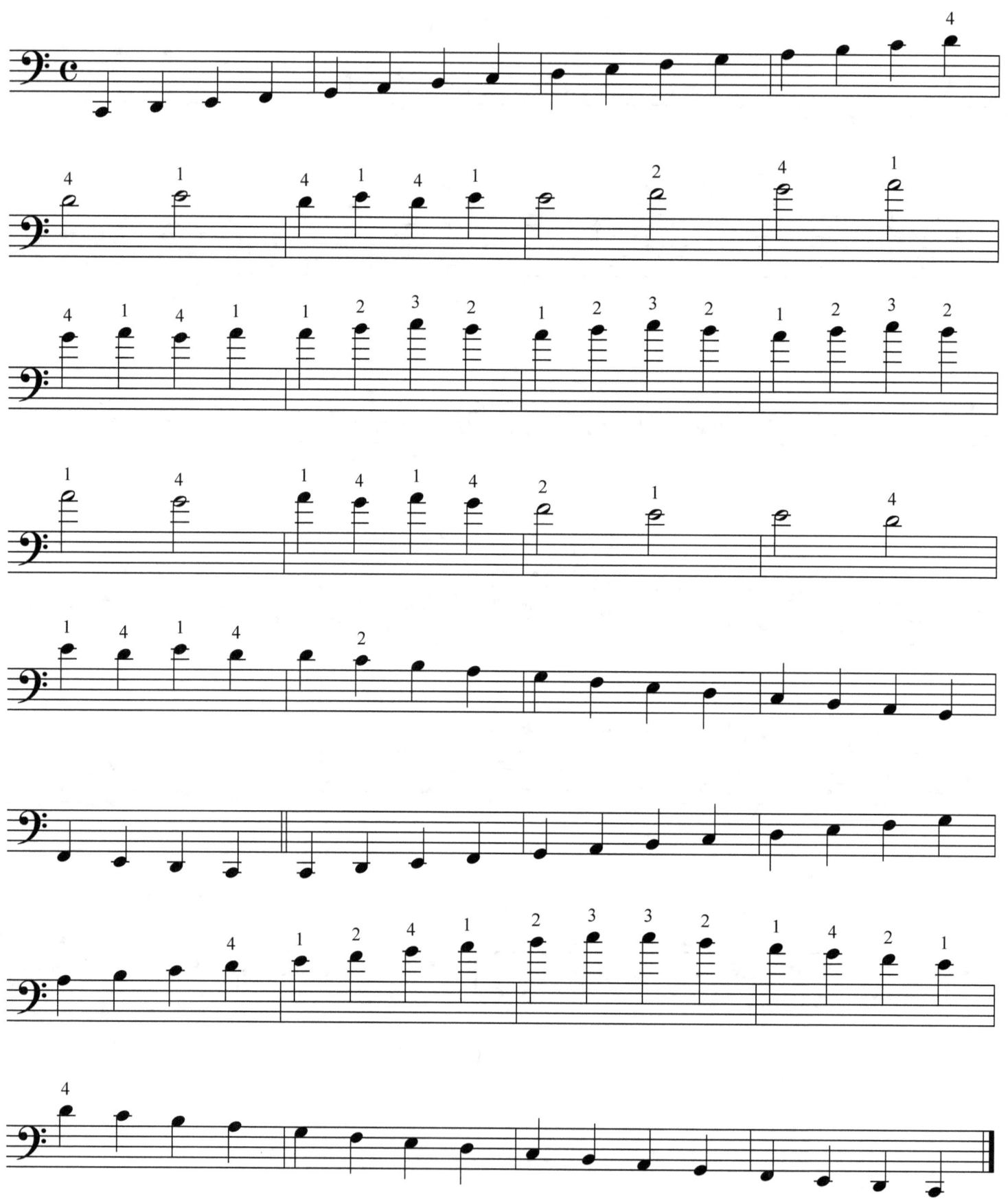

The C Major Scale Book for Cello

3

©2012 C. Harvey Publications All Rights Reserved.

4

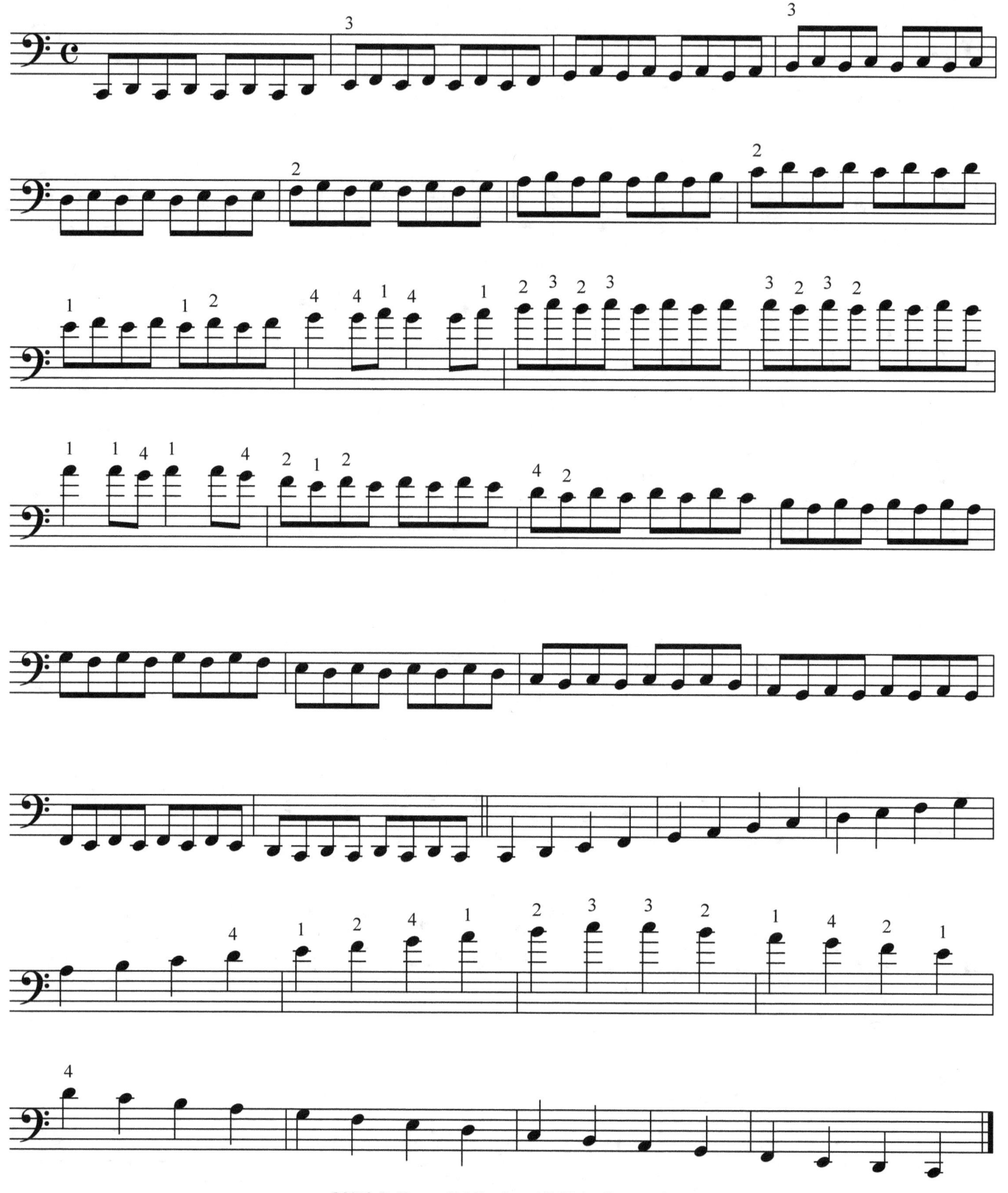

5

6

7

9

10

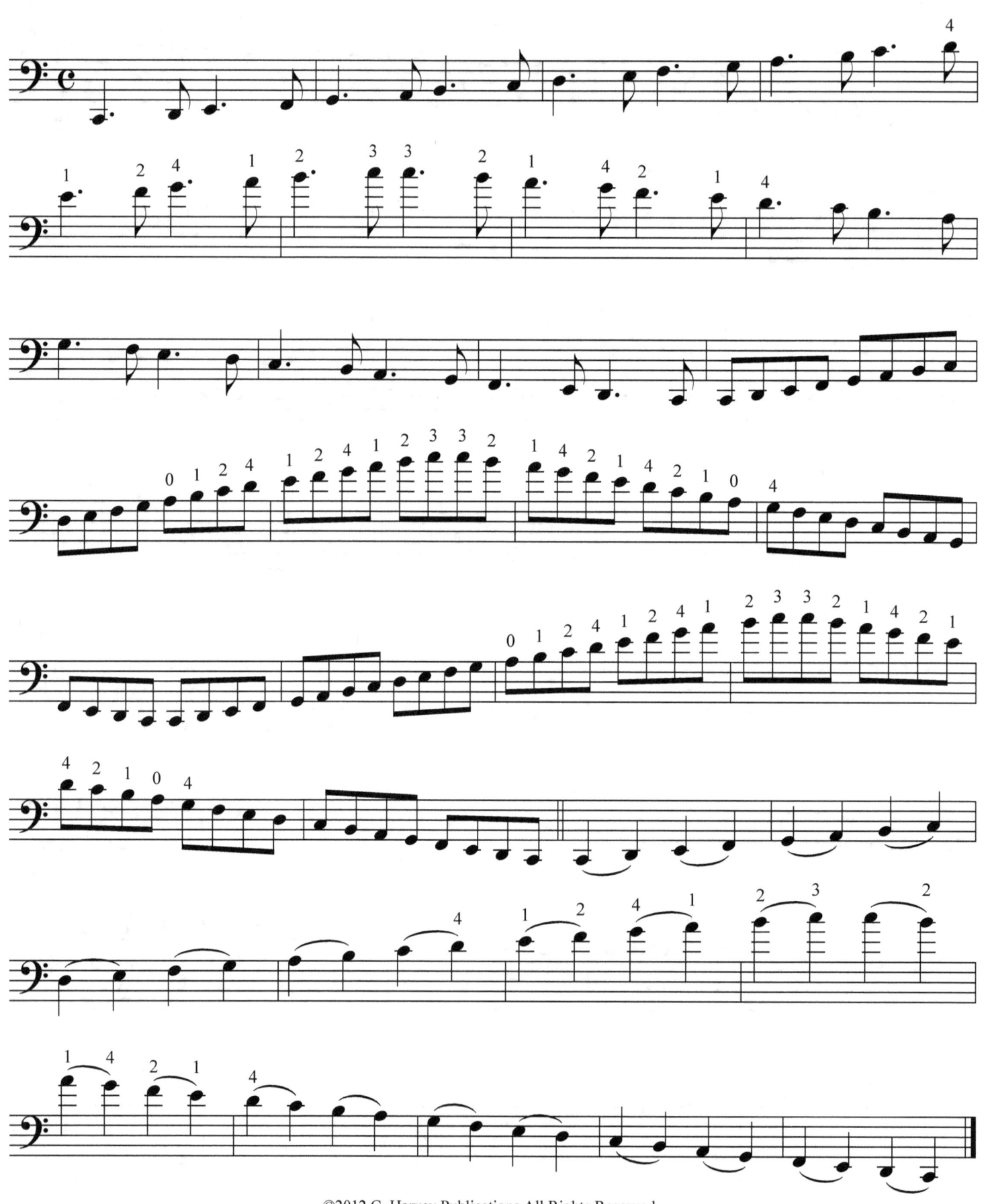

The C Major Scale Book for Cello

11

12

The C Major Scale Book for Cello

13

©2012 C. Harvey Publications All Rights Reserved.

14

15

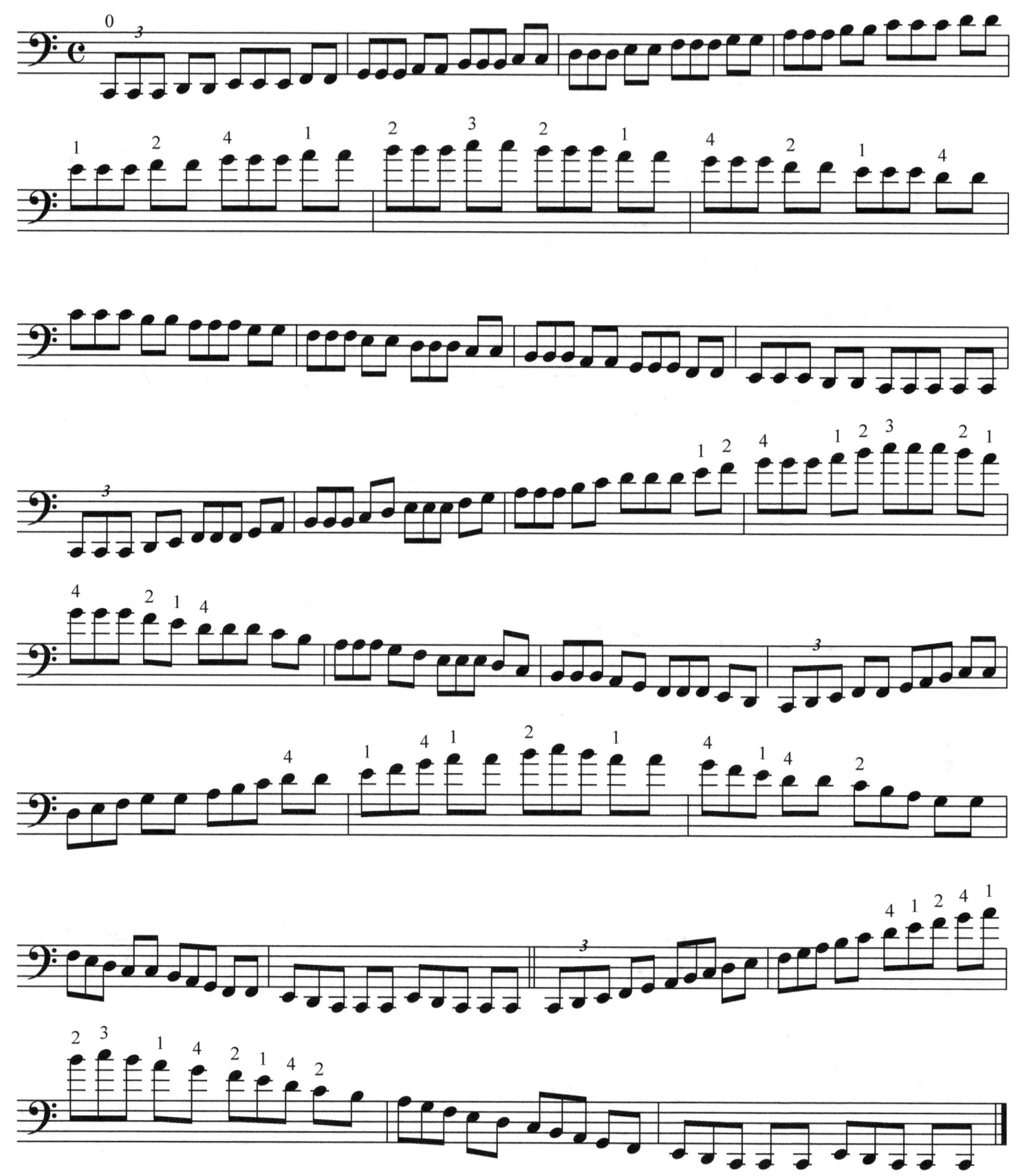

17

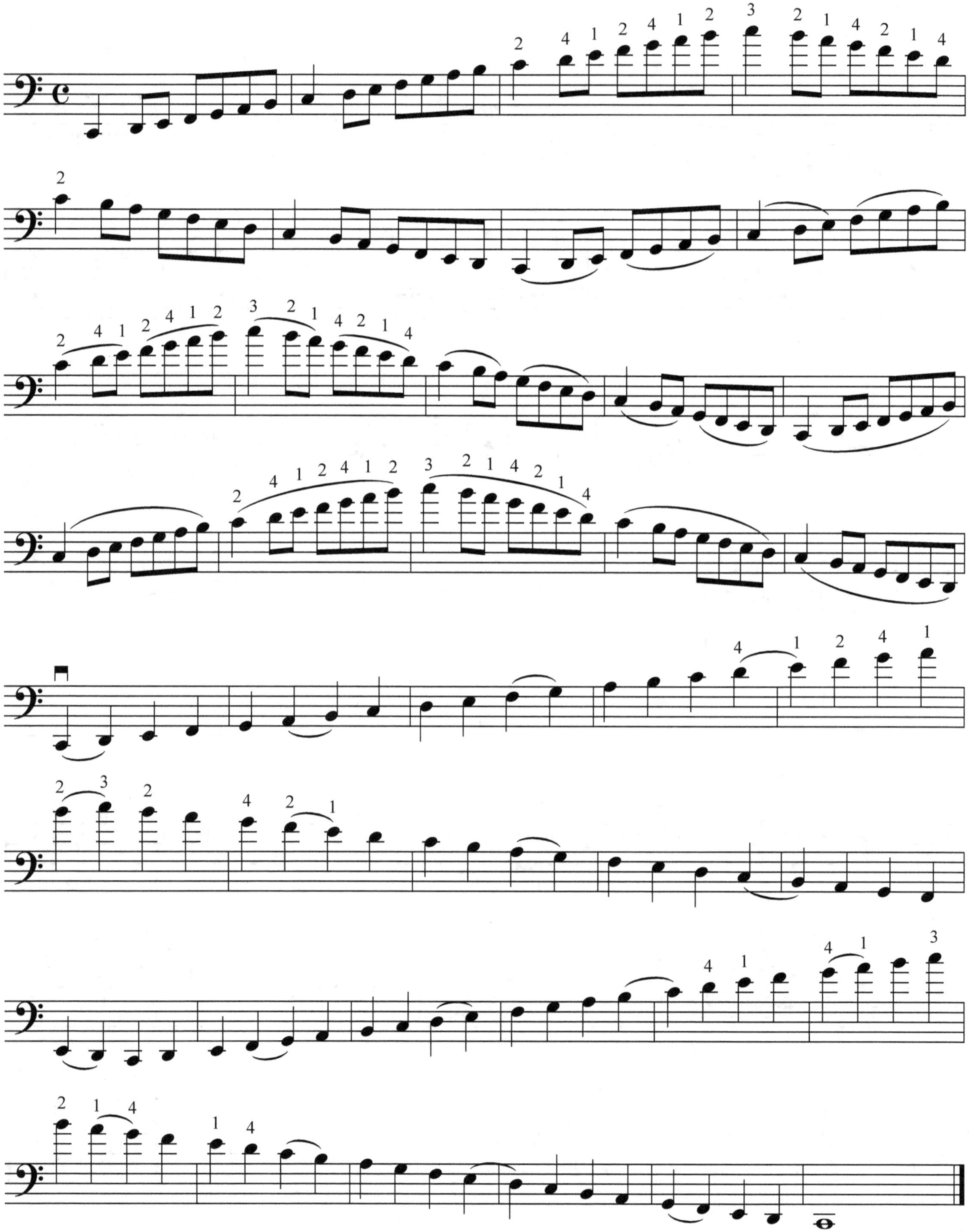

19

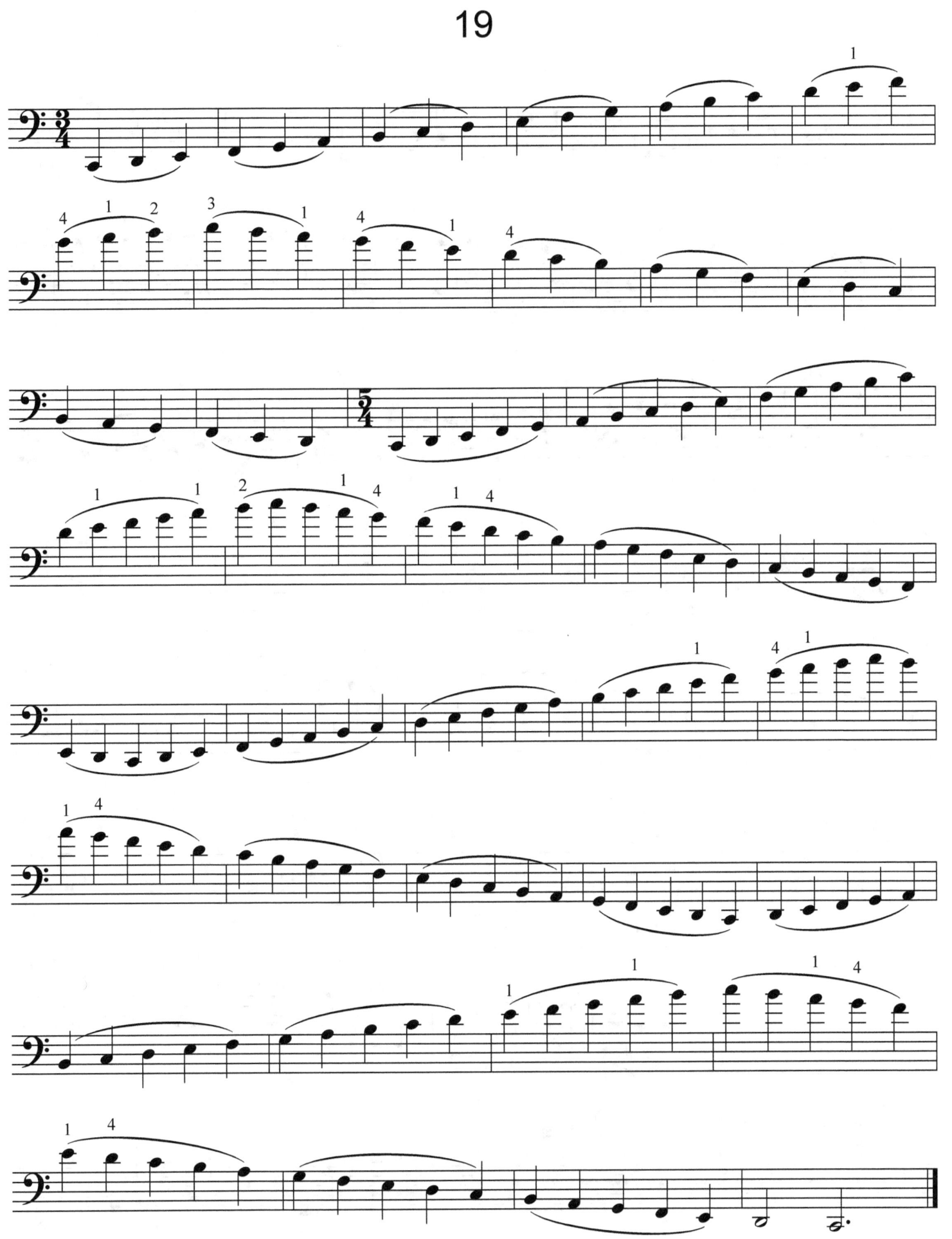

20

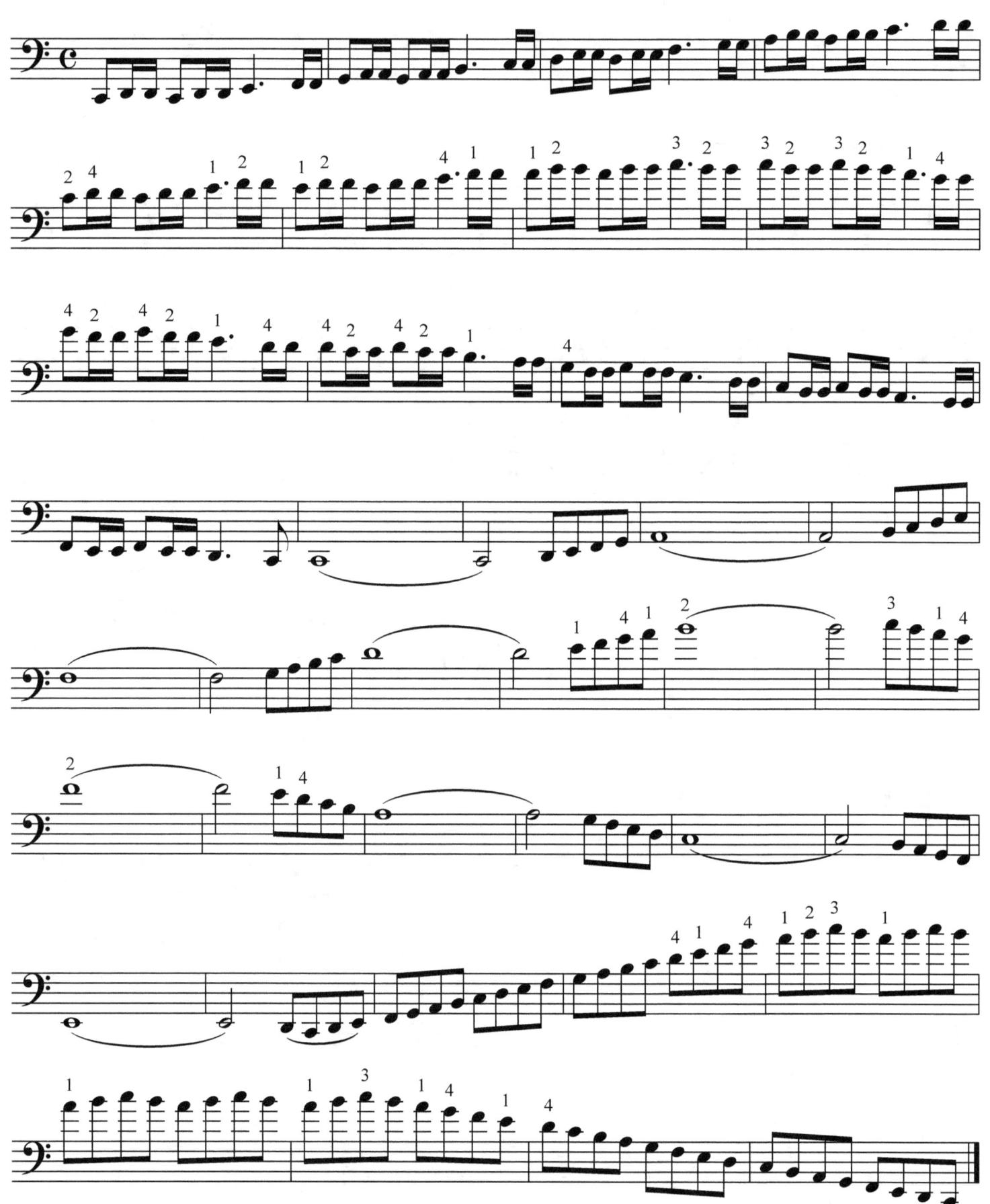

21

22

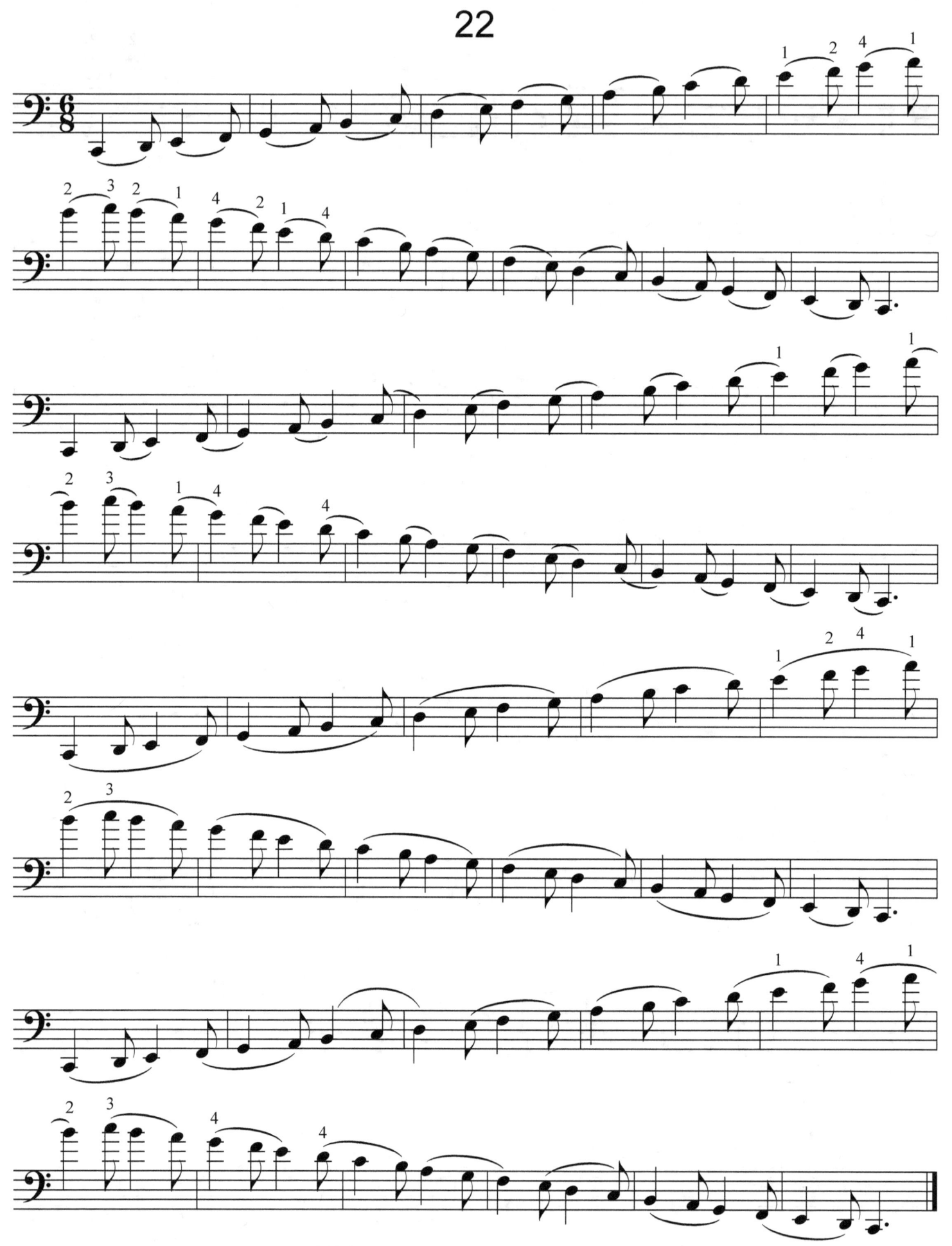

The C Major Scale Book for Cello

23

24

25

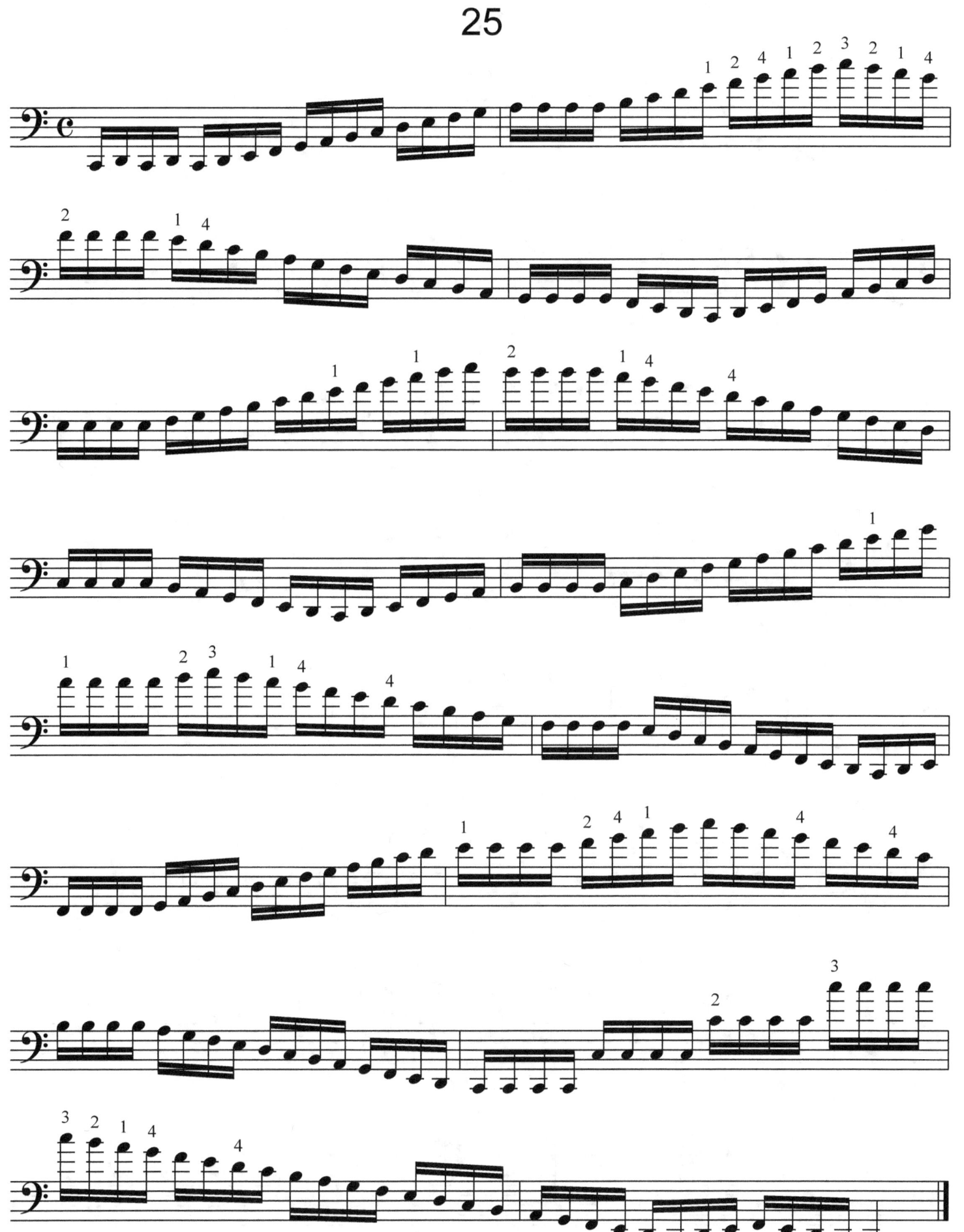

26

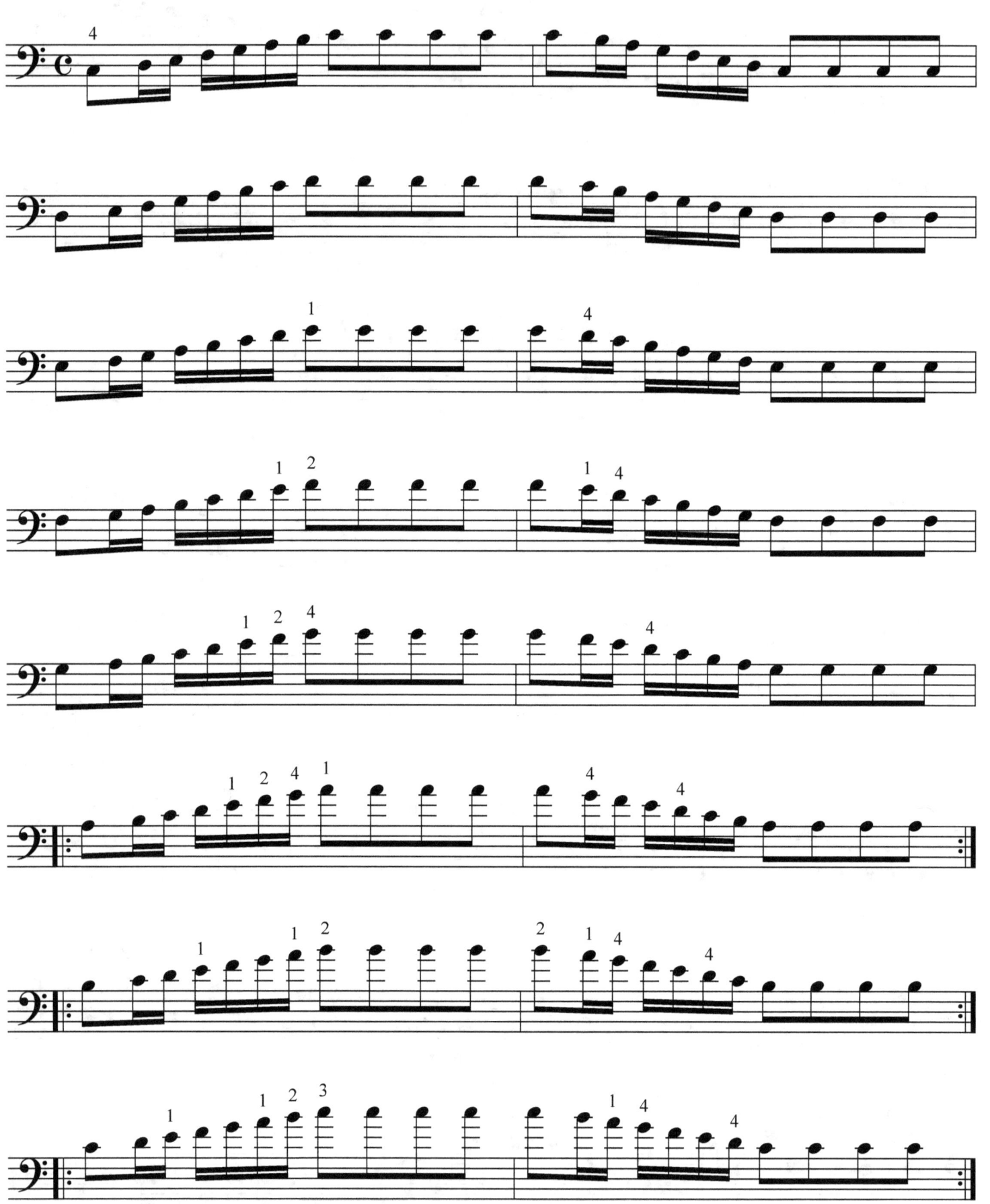

Also available from www.charveypublications.com: CHP356
Learning Three-Octave Scales on the Cello

Part One: Learning the Major Scales

C Major Scale

Cassia Harvey

©2019 C. Harvey Publications All Rights Reserved.

www.ingramcontent.com/pod-product-compliance
Lightning Source LLC
Chambersburg PA
CBHW051431070526
44584CB00023B/3677